Viva Bartali!

for

Bronwen Price
velocista

and

Matthew Williams
scalatore

Viva Bartali!

Damian Walford Davies

Seren is the book imprint of
Poetry Wales Press Ltd.
Suite 6, 4 Derwen Road, Bridgend, Wales, CF31 1LH
www.serenbooks.com
facebook.com/SerenBooks
twitter@SerenBooks

The right of Damian Walford Davies to be identified as
the author of this work has been asserted in accordance
with the Copyright, Designs and Patents Act, 1988.

ISBN: 9781781727089
Ebook: 9781781727096

A CIP record for this title is available from the British Library.

The publisher acknowledges the financial assistance of the Books Council of Wales.

Cover artwork: Gino Bartali at the Giro di Lombardia, 1952.

Contents

Ponte a Ema

Tuscany, 1924

You'd wake to the tang
of lye ash soap, to women singing

on the river bank, beating laundry
vestment-white and laying it to dry

like snow on furze and rock.
From bridge to ox-bow bend,

the pools were fishless, fizzing,
glib with suds. Some days,

what brought you round like salts
was Primo's dung cart, hauling

two weeks' worth from sties and coops
to strew across the flint-set fields.

Opening the shutters on a frozen street,
raffia iron-hard around the balcony,

you'd watch your father move
from lamp to lamp down Crucifixion Lane,

mount his ladder, snuff each sallow
oilflame with a shale-cut hand.

Vista

Florence, 1926

The ride to school was on a cast-off
butcher's bike, sin-black,

through lanes that dyed the tyres
white. You'd pass the blind man

on his daughter's doorstep
crying *Go, my boy!*, a girl

with wasted legs propped
puppet-like against a wayside shrine.

Then up the killing incline, scrip
rebounding off your back, along

a line of cypress flames until
the terracotta city opened out

before you at Piazza Michelangelo,
where blackshirts massed

below the copy of the *David*,
the manboy's weight thrown right,

a star of hair above the groin,
great lodes of blood across his hand.

Resurrection
Ponte a Ema, 1929

Midwinter afternoon, the cold
belligerent. A game of cops

and robbers, run all day in random
rat-tat-tats through barns

and steaming byres, gathered
to a shootout in the drifts

in Salvatore's field, snowball-bullets
ripping through the Boys in Blue.

Later, trailing moons of lantern glow
along the ground, Babbo

found you where the Scarface Swells
had tommy-gunned you down –

snow-sepulchred, heartbeat
hibernation-slow, a chrysalis

that took six months to thaw
to speech, *ragazzo*-Lazarus

who somewhere in that whiteout
promised never to be killed again.

Yolks

1933

Your summer regimen: dawn raid
on Babbo's hen-hutch, bantams

palmed aside for alabaster eggs
that clack inside your jersey's

pouch; a flask of ebony espressos
with the taste of cigarettes;

the weighed canteen of water, gram-
precise; your one spare tyre, torqued

figure-of-eight across your back;
goggles for the Tuscan dust;

three rattled-through Hail Marys
for the road. The morning full of grace –

gathered to the wicked slug of coffee
at the San Donato bend,

and your breaking of the shells
against the handlebars, eggwhites

trailing from the metal, gold hearts
wolfed down on your slick descents.

Amateur
1934

The tyke who'd trailed you
from the shabby starting flag

you knew from afternoons
in dim repair shops, where they hung

new tyres to cure like eels
above the bench-end vices

and the shining virgin cogsets
stacked like secret currencies.

In the final cobbled sprint –
pitched towards a May Queen

cradling flagging flowers
on a cock-eyed dais –

you let him have the mercy
of your slipstream, knowing

from the way he broke
he'd never make it past his cousin's

cast-off jersey and the pittance
of a feast-day parish purse.

Prayer

St Thérèse of Lisieux, 1873–97

St Thérèse, Little Flower –
keep us from the blind dog

blundering into our path;
the devils in the ruts; pride,

swaggering in victors'
yellow and pink. Be our shield

on broiling cols; steel us
for cloudburst and crosswind,

bullet-hail and brume's
deceptions. Shepherd us

through corridors of grasping
hands and gurning faces;

gird us in the peloton's
press; be lodestar on the lonely

breakaways. We have seen
Despair ride close beside us

on setts and cinderways.
Brace us; bring us home to flowers.

Succession

Giro d'Italia, 1935; Stage 6, Portocivitanova—L'Aquila, 25 May

Salt savour of the docklands start
still in your throat,

the foothills of the Sibyllines
were stringing out the riders'

starling flock, each hairpin
colder than the last. Past

Montemonaco, you found yourself
near Binda – hair immaculate

in bergamot and orange-oil
pomade, the crouch familiar

from your scrapbook galleries –
and dust-caked Girardengo,

flying pied in trademark black-barred
white, wee *campionissimo*.

You could have reached across
to touch them both, but kicked,

and climbing, logged their hands –
old gods', stippled brown with liver spots.

Anointing
Team Fréjus, 1935–6

You served base shifts
as bloodhound and aquarius –

reeling in pretenders, filling
team canteens at village pumps

and arrogant town fountains.
Evenings were in single rooms

in cheap hotels that smelled
of beefsteak, five lean frames

laid out on makeshift pallets,
suntans drawn in scalpel-lines

on arms and thighs, molasses–
dark. Through clouds of smoke

you watched the *soigneur*
knead the flesh with balsam

and dear spice, your pinstripe
Caraceni three-piece hanging

creaseless from the picture rail –
a risen body, ready to put on.

Adriana

Emporium '48', Via del Corso, Florence

In serge plus-fours the colour
of the sky behind the glazed

Madonnas, deadpan in their tondos
at the breakneck city junctions,

you'd ride across the Arno
on a clapped-out postie's bike

to stand outside and watch her
mouth her maths and lick

her middle finger, cashing up.
She'd let you run your palm

across the rolls of herringbone
and houndstooth, flannelette

and velveteen, and walk her
home, the bike wheeled chaste

between you, past the plaque
to crazy Filippo Argenti,

who shod his horse with silver,
charged it sparking down that street.

Martyr

Oratory of St Catherine of the Wheels, Ponte a Ema

You'd always stop here, prop
the bike against the kiln-hot pocked

façade and let the morning's speed
discharge to dust. Inside,

past broken harnesses,
dragon-toothed old harrows,

bodies of trapped birds,
you'd find sweet-muzzy fodder

stored in waves against the walls.
What mattered was the fresco

in the apse: the lanky girl-saint
yellow-frocked, moon-haloed,

blissfully at prayer, bound fast
between two wheels against

an umber sky – for all the world
a rider on the road to victory,

angels skirring down with palm fronds,
someone clapping madly at the back.

Solo

Team Legnano, Giro d'Italia, 1936; Stage 9, Campobasso–L'Aquila, 27 May

Lithe in ladykilling pink,
bronzed darling Gepin Olmo

with his filmstar widow's peak
sprang raging from the traps

at Campobasso. But you were
wolfish, too – snatching

at the shifter, mastering
the paradox of pedalling back

to prise dumb chainlinks
onto tighter sets of teeth,

your palm a burning blister
in the thinning buckskin glove,

a taste of lung-blood
in your mouth. On the pass

at Macerone, you were racing
no one but the goggled motorcade

and someone's shadow,
cubist on the roadside rock.

Tongue

Giro d'Italia, 1936; Stage 15a, Ferrara–Padua, 2 June

Across the maddening flatlands
broken only by day labour

standing scarecrow in the maize,
you thought of nothing

but that morning's thrilling girl
in gingham, doling out

pink newsprint like some work
of mercy from the sponsor's

open-topped saloon. Bergamaschi
crowed he'd come so close

he'd clocked her scent as Guerlain,
Vol de Nuit. You fixed your mind

around the relic on the duomo's
altar, coming closer with each

stroke: a saint's imperishable
tongue – pink still, unspeakable,

on feast days leeching wetness
under glass and gold.

Fiat 508 'Balilla'

Giulio Bartali, 20 October 1916–16 June 1936

What the driver saw, those last
half seconds on the blind bend's

darker side, across the bland
expanse of bonnet steaming

from the rain: two skyblue riders,
whippet-thin, tilting in a taut

ellipse as in a groove,
umbilical around the turn;

then another, jinking, fighting
with the camber, slamming in:

shock of brylcreemed hair,
car bucked sideways, carcass

jack-knifed by the mudguard's
breaking wave – bikeframe buckled,

somehow, in the radiator grille,
headlamps lighting poppies in the verge.

And God made the black Balilla –
that box coaxed, screaming, into curves.

Vault

Giro di Lombardia ('The Race of the Dead Leaves'), 8 November 1936

Flashbulb laps inside the velodrome
before the buffed track's

slingshot camber flung you north
past Monza's smokestacks, through

the suburbs of the textile plants.
Beyond to Como, cattle churned

the fields to mire, greying corn cobs
on the verges like grenades.

On the lakefront, cowboy Marabelli
with the star-patch on his pocket

toyed with you through loops of mist.
Scaling the Ghisallo, eyes soldered

to the belfry on the hill, you knew
the brute climb's only wages was

the sight of roadside sepulchres –
del Rossi, Verri, Chiaravalli

on their lintels, dark *tifosi* clapping
from beyond the iron grilles.

Glacial

Training ride, Florence–Milan–Florence (330km), March 1937

Pineland – high, south-east
of Cento Croci; wolfland –

feral winter through to May.
Did you feel the air warm

just enough to make the haze
clot, anvil-grey, between the boles,

then chill again to let the flakes
come slantwise, needle-cold?

You pushed on blind to Serpiano,
gasping at the ashen-angel's

raw French kiss, the water
in your bidon cracking into ice

until the sky became ceramic blue
at Pian del Falco, and the dumb-

found farmhand leading oxen
into shelter saw a frostman

take the turn at Via Passerino,
trailing crystals like a comet tail.

Revenant

Giro d'Italia, 1937; Stage 16, Vittorio Veneto–Merano, 26 May

High day in the Dolomites,
grand tors like bombed basilicas.

On the Costalunga you were out
alone – the rest wrung ragged

on the valley floor, the soldier
on the growling Moto Guzzi

smoking, side-tracked by the view,
not noticing the sweet dead boy

who paced you beautifully
in last June's dimming colours,

towed you up the pass
as on an iron cable, taut

between you, gear and cadence
matched, his breathless lungs

yours too to breathe in,
till he turned to smile, and falling

back, released you for the summit,
slung you crying hard downwind.

Maglia Rosa

Pink Jersey, Giro d'Italia, 1937; Grand Hotel, San Pellegrino Terme

Not pink, exactly; certainly
not white – the warm, just-laundered

jersey on a bed of crêpe,
delivered to your room by manager

and maître d'. You laid it
on the chest of drawers and lit

an evening cigarette. Tinned
salmon? Flesh, if slightly flushed?

Light altered off the river, close
outside. Paler now – the colour

of the sow that Babbo led
each autumn on a running noose

from sty to outhouse,
where the rootless knifeman

shaved her, stropped the knife,
then stuck her as you raised the hind legs

high, dazzled by the lustre
of the fast arterial flood.

23

Order
Italian Cycling Federation committee, June 1937

Nine, all smoking; four in uniform;
a woman at the stenograph,

hair crimped like Myrna Loy's.
On the wall: Il Duce – nervy

on a pushbike – next to kestrel-
faced Starace on a stallion, caught

mid-vault across the bonnet of a car;
and six-foot, sullen Graziani,

taking the salute of *bersaglieri*, south
of Addis Ababa. Agenda item two

was you. They called you *fraticello*,
little monk, questioned how

your ice-cut lungs were faring,
weighed three doctors' letters

recommending rest. Then the order –
curter than the fingers' shorthand;

on black lapels, the axe blade
in the *fasces* cutting to the chase.

Jordan

Tour de France, 1937; Stage 8, Grenoble–Briançon, 8 July

Nothing – the wireless crooned –
so fine as you on Ballon d'Alsace.

But *L'Auto*'s yellow newsprint
dyed all jerseys *jaune*. No one heard

the gattling crackle of your lungs
above the tyres' gutturals

on gravel tracks, the grind of engines
stuck in first. *Viva Gino!* screamed

a weeping roadside rock; helix
bends turned stomachs inside out.

Tearing free of Embrun in a mizzle,
close in Guido Rossi's draught,

you saw his back wheel yaw;
how slow it was, how slow – steel

buckling and your slingshot fall
across the quincunx rivets of the bridge

to be baptised again, the torrent
making glacial whirlpools of your blood.

Commune

Giulio Bartali's grave, Ponte a Ema

Spring evenings, osiers yellow
on the towpath stabbing into leaf,

you'd wind your brother's rosary
about your wrist, the thin tin Christ

pressed hard into your palm,
black beads like coffee beans,

and take the route the coffin took,
remembering the white chrysanthemums

held out at doorways as your mother
passed, to pick your way

through candleflames in jam jars,
sputtering on graves, towards the loggia

and the highbacked chair you'd kneel on
at the wall of tall, stacked vaults,

eyeline level through the oil lamp's
chainlinks with the lead-grey letters

of his name, the 'O' all lack, all hollow,
but rolling perfect like a wheel.

Vicarious

9 May 1938; Hitler visits Florence; stage 3 of the Giro d'Italia

That spring you kicked your heels.
All day you hovered tetchy

round the tombstone wireless,
cranking through the channels'

gears for news. At noon from Genoa:
Gotti dropped Leoni north of Celle

on the bay-lit riviera road.
From Florence: high, clipped voices

conjured boot-black cavalcades,
salutes from balconies,

ringfenced stop-offs in piazzas
grey with guns. When the cars

purred up to Santa Croce's steps
you closed your eyes,

picturing the pageant
from the vantage of the high façade

where the statue of the Virgin
had a sniper's deadeye view.

Posy

Ponte a Ema

Waiting for your ride,
dressed ritzy – spearpoint collar,

wingtip brogues, great clouts
of French cologne still burning

on your cheeks, your gilt Movado
ticking heavy on your wrist –

you watched your father
walking home along the plumb-

flush windrows of the far
alfalfa fields, a nightjar churring

in the headland like a spinning wheel.
Beyond the gate, June ground

exhaled a stage-prop vapour,
rash as grappa fumes.

He strode towards you smiling,
asked what time it was,

holding out a spray of flowers:
simple purples for your mother's sills.

Capitano

Tour de France, 1938; Pavillon Henri IV Hotel, 3 July

On the breakfast terrace, Paris
broiling on the skyline east,

a king's parterres in arabesques
and monograms below,

you posed the team's eleven
in a trim diminishing line

like chorus girls, pressmen held at bay
by bellhops tensing tasselled

curtain cords, and for the photo
stepped inside the slender breach

you'd kept between the scapula
of Bergamaschi and clavicle

of Servadei. Next morning's *L'Auto*
led with ladykiller Aldo Bini's larks,

a piece devoted to your scowl
and tight shots of your face and arms:

skeins of veins like hawsers,
on your boxer's nose the sunburst scar.

Dog

Tour de France 1938; Stage 8, Pau–Luchon, 14 July

You caught them saddle-napping
at Eaux-Chaudes – tickled

by the fatmen in their diapers
on the terrace of the spa –

and bolted like a gazehound,
only Vissers and Vervaecke

kicking with you up the scree,
the mad fairweather masses

thinning at each bend.
On the Tourmalet, the fight was with

hurt's angel, mind untwisting
on the coiling track, dust-throat

mocked by pilsner on the billboards
out of Louderville. On the Peyresourde

a girl in vichy-check ran out to snatch
a dachshund from the road; she left

your leg like bacon, all-black Vissers
and Vervaecke plunging past.

Peau

Tour de France, 1938; Stage 14, Col d'Izoard, 22 July

From the dustcloud belly
of the baggage train, a megaphone

bawled out your lead in cracked
Italian through the moonscape

of the Casse Déserte. There was
time enough to notice

how a fine grey dust descended
on your arms, like mamma's

sifted flour from a sack
the colour of the Virgin's cloak,

parching then to snakescale
crust, sweat slaking it to clay

until the staggered watchers
at the summit saw a man of ash

thrash past, his face a mask,
and wished him such a steeping

at Briançon as would be
the utter shedding of a skin.

Assumption

Tour de France, 1938; rest day, Aix-les-Bains, 24 July

At meals you'd stand her
near your wineglass – girl-faced,

peeling, wood Madonna, pocket-size –
and watch her watching you

mouth grace and cross yourself
then rout a chicken to the ribcage,

osso buco to its coin of bone.
At the pavement tables, evening

bleaching off the lake, no one noticed
how, through four espressos

and their sister-cigarettes,
you inched her forward on the cloth

before the hounding line of shadow
hungry to eclipse her hem –

and how you kept her bathed
in sunlight till you raised her,

kissed her, brushed the ash-flecks
from her saw-toothed crown of stars.

Choice

Tour de France 1938; final stage, Lille–Paris, 31 July

Two yellow jerseys
on the stripped-back bed in Lille,

laid side-by-side. Yesterday's
dried stiff with grease and sputum,

sweat and Picardy's green
clay, your fading number inked

in stencil on the ragtag card.
The other fresh and flawless,

puckered tight at sleeves
and neckline, '13' pulsing sharp

and lucky on a fresh white field.
In the Sunday tiers of the Parc

des Princes, they craned to cheer
an idol flaring in, impeccable;

what they got was more a thing
of iron, grinding out

the last kilometer, sullied shirt
a distant shade of gold.

Dedication

Church of Our Lady of Victory, Paris, 31 July 1938

They hemmed you in against
the hoardings, notepads cocked.

Questions came like grapeshot;
you snarled ripostes. They pointed

to the peacock's tail of blooms
you'd shouldered on your lazy

showboat laps — whipped-cream
roses, dense chrysanthemums, lilies

threatening to undress. *Pretty flowers,
Gino — for Il Duce, eh?* You offered them

a desiccated smile. Morning had you
suited near the Seine, moving fast

up Rue du Louvre, presspack
tracking in the scent trail

of your grand bouquet. In the still
basilica, you laid it at the alabaster

Virgin's feet, lilies' trembling anthers
shedding burnt sienna on your cuffs.

Publicity

Piazza del Duomo, Florence; August 1938

They wheeled you out in yellow,
posed you, buttressed, on the bucktooth

cobbles of the square, feet fast
inside the pedals' cages, hunkered

on your handlebars. Each bulbflash volley
washed your oiled hair white.

They sent you clockwise round
the duomo, talked you into tearing

back again, teeth bared, to take
a seat behind a sculpted table

brokered from a banker's rooms
and sign, all afternoon, the ziggurats

of cards until the line gave out at six
with Giotto's bells. For the child

in wooden splints you drew a massif
of serrated peaks, yourself the small,

capped stickman on the last ascent –
gravity-confounding, somehow hanging on.

Mass

Cardinal Elia Dalla Costa, Archbishop of Florence

You'd watch him, birdlike
at the altar, doused in watered silks,

skin drawn sheer across
a jawing skull, oversized *mozzetta*

spread like scarlet wings
at every effort of the arms.

Your Sunday collar chafed.
On your knees, hands clinched

above the chancel rail, you waited
for a body in a brittle wheel

of bread, blood-gouts in a giddy
nip of wine. In prayer again,

you tracked a flogged man's
climb along a narrow street,

the baying crowds, the lungburst
at the crest, screams

leavened by the creaking
of the red bird's Ferragamo shoes.

Headline

Italian fascist Manifesto of Race, 1938

Jackboots beat the bounds down
Borgo Ognissanti, black berettas

snug in sleek hide holsters, trigger fingers
nervous at the clips. You'd spend

your rest days at Fantoni's, pouring
landslide dunes of sugar on the paper

tablecloth to map tomorrow's
climbs. That morning in the skint

November sun, *Corriere della Sera's*
headline barefaced on the banning

of the Jews, the sports page
raving over Michelini's strikes,

you crossed to view the long
Last Supper in the sideroom

of All Saints, where in the blue
beyond the *trompe l'oeil* arches,

gamebirds nosedive out of nowhere,
tilting earthwards, fat as bombs.

Signs

Milan–San Remo ('The Spring Classic'), 19 March 1939

St Joseph's Day but with a polar
wind, the duomo's finials

lancing flurries from a low-slung
Lombard sky. In a field

past Siccomario, fifty sidecar rigs
in dead-matt grey. At Ilva Spa

a woman baying in a wheelchair
in a plot of pears. On the bridge

at Santo Criste, children clouting
trout against the balustrade.

Beyond the Pass at Fado Alto
foxes nailed along a fence. At Cagoleto

in a filthy yard, a grinning man in oil-
skins, grinding knives. Near

Capo Berta, vistas of a void,
gunmetal sea. At the bunch-sprint

finish line, they wound you
in a sheet that cinched you like a shroud.

Acolyte

Giro d'Italia, 1940; Fausto Coppi 1st, Bartali 9th

You'd expected swagger, bluster,
just-turned-twenty balls – a bruiser

in your livery to be your windbreak
wall. But the boy was pigeon-

chested, heron-shanked – a lanky
butcher's lackey with a Piedmont

drawl. In the spittledust near
Genoa, your hammered elbow

blooming to a bruise, you waved him
madly onwards, learning later

how he'd soloed, lightning-lit,
through oakwoods, gulping static

with a slackjaw gape. Then to find him,
through a four-day fug of foodbags

touted out of reach, in pink and panicked,
spewing on the verge; so you played

the father, pressing snowdrift to his temples
till it ran in runnels to his shins.

Draft

October 1940, call up: motorcycle messenger,
Lake Trasimeno, Umbria

You traded nappa mitts for gauntlet
gloves; training rides' great loops

for point-to-point dispatches, learned
salutes; the mantra of your breathing

for an engine's grunt. There were days
of nothing more than writing home

with barricades of kisses, softening up
new packs of playing cards

and bartering smokes. One Sunday
in the shelter of a stand of pines

at Sant'Arcangelo, rain like grapeshot
in the reeds, you watched them lug

a pike ashore – a foot of skull, in perfect
combat camouflage. In the creel it thrashed

and flexed above the bed of perch
and tench until the gills were still,

mouth a grim insinuation of a smile,
amber irises like wedding rings.

Marriage

to Adriana Bani, 14 November 1940;
conducted by Cardinal Dalla Costa

He set your rings to touch
along his service book's split spine,

reeling off a murky riff on how
the Father in a godforsaken garden

laid the Son asleep and drew
salvation like a woman

from his wound. Obedient,
your hand in hers, you tried to follow

but were waylaid by the razorline
of light that bleached his cheek

and inched across his rochet's
bobbin lace to start a slow

incineration of her wedding dress
and scorch her veil apart to leave you

dropped, astonished, stranded
in the flatfoot time between

two gears – the kiss you bent to
velvet as a home-strait shifting up.

Present

Jewish family Goldenberg

Armando Sizzi! 'Mando! Dove sei?
The shop was dark. You called your cousin

from his workshop den. He entered
grinning, grease cloths wrung through

belt loops, bike tubes like bright
femurs in his fist. He ragged you

on your photo card – the studied
racing pose; the comb's confection

of a quiff; glossed lips to rival
Clara Calamai's. You turned the talk

to Fiesole on the hill – the hushed
stone house that friends were breaking

bread in, watching for the ad hoc black
patrols. For the son you scrawled a card

and picked a bike; drove it up
the pitted climb past vine rows,

pruners at their summer surgery,
tendrils' green antennae in their trugs.

Blue

Fausto Coppi's victories: Giro di Toscana, 1941;
National Road Race, 1942; the Hour Record, 1942

Losing had a dull metallic taste
the evening's chain of cigarettes

could never clear. The boy was
gawky still but spun a faultless

cadence from each climb. He'd traded
green for slick Bianchi's blue;

milling round at starting lines,
you'd smell him first: heady liniment

of wintergreen the blind Cavanna
boiled to baste him in. All things

stung: how he turned his 's's
in his autographs; how a sleek

black forelock fell across his face;
those orbs of eyes; the way he'd simply

done without you in the velodrome –
whirred an hour's ride between

two bouts of Yankee bombing,
racing no one but the countdown clock.

Nocturne

September 1943: Italy surrenders to the Allies; German occupation

Late smokes in your strip of garden,
herb bed dizzy with the day's

stowed heat. You heard your son
cry out in nightmare, wail on waking

to a blinding dark. She brought him out
to moonlight, trusting sage and thyme

would be a balm. You held him,
crooning – pointed up to Draco

coiled between the Bears. Your trinities
of sweet pea canes cast latticed

shadows on the still-warm wall.
A moth was beating in the scabious,

pallid on the purple blooms. You bent
to look – so close your son could see

the feathered legs and silver eyes,
turned perfectly like collar studs.

He screamed, delivered from a horror
only to be hagged by horror once again.

Screen

Nuvole, Umbria; October–November 1943

From front-page phiz to this:
a bolthole in a perishing high place,

a borrowed name, an outsize cap
rammed low. Some days were with

the farmer docking beets, observing
how the mists could lift in seconds,

like a curtain going up, to show
grey theatres of trucks across

the Tiber flats. By five you'd plash
indoors through quilts of cattle breath;

by six you'd all be swaddled by the fire –
the boy asleep, your Adriana

clapping blood awake in cast-off
soldier's gloves, cured beechwood

cracking silence like a gun. Chancing
it one Sunday, you were rumbled

in the dim confessional – raw denials
falling through the fretwork on deaf ears.

Commission

Cardinal Dalla Costa, Archbishop's Palace, Florence, November 1943;
request from the Delegation for the Assistance of Jewish Emigrants

He'd called you early, knowing
how the SS death's-heads

annexed café tables, sharp at eight,
rapping zippos on the marble tops.

He met you gaunt, unchaperoned,
tidemarked scarlet set aside

for shirt and slacks. In the study,
echoes dampened by the books,

he drew a map of Jews in basements,
cloisters, attic rooms – ghosts

policing breath in back-cracked dark
the other side of wainscots, waiting

for the papers that would forge them
into flesh again. He conjured courier-

angels, quizzed you hard on gradients
and riding times. Dazed, you crossed

a chill piazza, waiters in Scudieri's
in their clear-cut black and white.

Drop
Florence; November 1943

Absurd, you thought: a pallid moon;
the river staging spookish coils

of mist; a cat's slashed scream.
Where the bank surrenders

to a shingle beach, a priest
was leaning on the parapet, pompom

of his black biretta like your son's
cot toy. You drew your cap down

close. He broke your stride by asking
for a light; you wavered, pulse

at climbing pace. He took a nervous
drag, leaned in again to whisper:

He that watcheth over Is-ra-el
shall slumber not, nor sleep.

He handed over photographs –
ten strangers in a cheapjack

bracelet box. *You're the ark,*
he offered. *Curl them like a scroll.*

Diversion

Terontola train station, Tuscany; December 1943

Always, tricks and timing: when
to kick; how to mount a phoney

rallentando; when to feign a shunt
in gear. On the overpass, you fixed

a phantom flat that let you scan
the platforms, listen for the railpulse

of the northbound 2:14. At 2:08
you staged a bright annunciation

in the bar, pitched perfectly between
event and bonhomie, the bike

a glowing lure. You downed a glass
of wine and let them paw you,

led them in a *Gi-no! Gi-no!* chant
that brought the grey police

in silver gorgets running in. You took
your own sweet time to chew

the tissue-thin *prosciutto*. Outside,
ten people very quietly changed trains.

Cache

Father Rufino Niccacci (Assisi underground network);
monastery of San Damiano, Assisi, December 1943

Your knocking had a Luger's dull report
that sent the doves in circles, brought

the slap of sandals down the stairs.
His sackcloth was the russet

of turned fields. You followed to a dim
refectory; against the trestles,

still-life vases, lumpen putti in a low
lunette, the bike was business

from another world. He watched you
shimmy off the saddle, draw a whorl

of faces from the tube and lay them
in his missal to be pressed like

blooms. At the gate he asked
what else your bright machine's insides

might store; you joked you'd fill her up
with scotch. He blessed you,

noting, deadpan, that the sky
had blanched a true Bianchi blue.

49

Aubade

Via del Bandino, Florence; January 1944

Waking to a caustic cold, frail
counterpane rucked up

around her hip, you noticed
how her breath kept tempo

with the ticking of the clock.
There was light enough to see

your own breath come in clouds;
the water in the ewer

had the slimmest film of ice. Long
johns, woollens, jersey, jacket,

Longines watch; then mittens
over mittens and the skull cap

with the surging 'B' she'd conjured
in the after-supper silence

as you smoked. She stirred;
you knew she knew that what

you'd donned was battledress
the days you left her in the dark.

Ruota

Communication 'wheel'; San Quirico convent (Assisi underground network);
February 1944

Above the door, a bright *Madonna*
of the Milk, her mantle parted

for the Child to pluck the palest
pomegranate of a breast. The bell

pull burned you, stiff with frost.
The rest was done in silence

and near-dark: your shy boy's nod;
the schlepp down cross-lined halls

behind the Madre in her dazzling
coif; the rite around the hollow

drum they spun as door between
two worlds. You watched it roll;

inside, the forger's miracles:
fantasies of card and photo film,

glued seals and Gentile surnames
lifted from a southern postal book –

dearer then than any saint's parched
relics, torpid in a jewelled box.

Cellar

Goldenberg family; Via del Bandino, Florence, April 1944

You moved them underground
among the demijohns, contrived

a bed from pallets, sheets
from hessian sacks. On your rides

you'd picture them in darkness –
parsing street noise up to

curfew, learning stillness,
stifling coughs. Food you stuffed

in pockets, bluffed inside
your race *musette*. It was eyes

you saw on entering: the boy's
dark reservoirs, the mother's

blue like bombers' Bengal lights.
You spoke in crude charades,

the stockpiled silence louder
than the air raid siren's

wail, your lantern casting
golem shadows on the wall.

Strafe

Bastia Umbra, Umbria; June 1944

Ninety in the shade; all objects
spectral; the long piazza laid asleep.

You filled your bottle at the fountain –
blistered iron, torquing to a griffon's beak.

The heat was like a flail. You recognised
the drone – pulsed baritone of English

engines closing from the east. Beyond
the rose-and-cream confection a church

you caught a smack of coffee on the air
but missed the sunflash off your bike's

bare forks. It drew two lines of knee-jerk
fire – raking parallels that smashed the slabs

to shrapnel, brought the café windows down
like waterfalls. The plane howled past –

so low you saw the crosses of the pilot's
kills. Still the long piazza slept.

You hurried south through cover,
stopping only to baptise the bike in dust.

Pastoral

German detachment, Monticchiello, Val D'Orcia, Tuscany;
June 1944

Seeing smoke too late, you rode
straight into them – blond hair

run crazy into curls, scuffed jackboots
pale with dust, unbuttoned jackets

missing epaulettes. Boys, they barred
the road, closed round to read

the name embroidered on your shirt.
Then, supplicants, they held out scraps

of card for autographs, moved close
to pet the leather on the ram-horn

handlebars. All smiles, you asked them
not to touch, so fine the tuning. Two more

were busy at the hedgeline, torching
hives. The plaited straw resisted first,

then fired with a honeyed trace.
They led the farmer on a shabby horse

to view the cones of fire; bees burst
like bullets from the flames.

Charity

Interrogation by Major Mario Carità: 'Villa Triste', Florence;
July 1944

So the summons came – not barked
or whispered but, absurdly, printed

on a card. You knew the place. How then
to play it, as you passed the grilles

that let the basement's howls escape
to echo in the bourgeois street? You waited

in the hall; someone struck up Schubert
in a far-off room. A girl played Virgil, led you

down until the carpets turned to coal dust,
stucco flaked to stone. On the bunker's table,

blood like sediment of wine. He entered
ranting that the Virgin was a whore.

Through blinding light and bouts of dark
you plied a simple storyline. That night

you heard him maim a man; the next,
the marred man's whimpering. In the morning,

drunk, he let you walk, announced he was
the angel who had rolled away the stone.

Break

Florence; August 1944

You watched her prowl the garden,
rub her drum-tight belly

with both palms. It was evening
when her waters broke. Busy

setting pots to boil, her mother
sent you riding late past refugees

and ruins, brazier flames and strays,
to knock on doctors' doors

and beg. You returned to candles
and a tiny thing: skin transparent,

buds of toes, a smile. All decorous,
all still. Priestless, it was you

who'd take the little cist through blitzed
and trash-filled streets and place it

by the casket of your brother.
At bay the week before

they'd blown the bridges, left the Arno
like a mouth of busted teeth.

Oddments

Piazzale Loreto, Milan; 29 April 1945

You'd ridden north to root
for scavenged steel, patched rubber,

suede or leather, nuts and bolts.
It was the crowd's electric drone

that drew you to the square
to find the thrashed cadavers

hanging by their heels like divers
checked mid-plunge: Petacci's skirt

rigged modestly around her thighs,
arms out as if to catch another

on her death trapeze; Bombacci
twirling like a fairy in a music box;

Il Duce, slimmer than the man
in photographs, botched face

a bowl of curds. The bikeframe
grounded you. Starace's belly juddered

as they yanked him up; below
there was a fleeting scuffle for his shirt.

Superannuate

Milan–San Remo, 19 March 1946; Coppi 1ˢᵗ, Bartali 4ᵗʰ, +18 minutes

Adrift? You knew so at Voghera –
Ortelli bouncing like a puppydog,

Leoni brutal, lionish. The road rose
slyly at Ovada as the flanking woods

came down. Then, the winnowing –
the years like grab-hooks on your

muscles, twists of alien pain.
From there it was a day you'd simply

read about: how the war-long
tunnel at Turchino birthed

a heron-man who flew the coast
in loneliness, so fast he stopped

to take a coffee in a small-town
bar, the wireless killing time

with music till an also-ran
rolled in, Swiss margins ditched

for broad-brush timing
from the church's quarter bell.

Renaissance

Giro d'Italia 1946, 'Il Giro della Rinascita' – The Giro of Rebirth;
Bartali 1ˢᵗ, Coppi 2ⁿᵈ

They sent you south across
the old map's battlelines,

north past years of soldiers'
graves. Send-offs were in

spruced piazzas, barked by
chains of modish mayors.

Beyond the bunting: bombed-out
backstreets, unbridged rivers,

rags and dogs. The road was
strewn with roses out of Prato,

Slavic nails at breakaway
Trieste. In a field at Trento,

women waving on a blistered tank;
rail tracks at Chieti rearing up

like mammoth tusks. Crabby,
older now, you ground a resurrection

from the mountains, the young
republic colic in its crib.

Benediction

Giro d'Italia, 1946; riders' delegation blessed by Pope Pius XII,
Rome, 25 June

They kept you waiting in an anteroom
beyond an anteroom, marble floors

like skating rinks. Outside, eternal
parapets and close-curled

prophets' heads, pigeons detonating
into blue. You watched them fidget –

Coppi ratcheting a ring; the way
Ortelli played his brakes

in time with some internal tune;
Ronconi fumbling with his tie's

botched knot. Buzzers sounding,
bolts shot back. Then he was

among you – icy, columnar –
a breakaway of chaplains keeping pace,

the scripted blessing trembling
in the trick vibrato's trill. Herded

out, you caught Ortelli winking
at a baked-earth bust of Habbakuk.

Plea

14 July 1948: Tour de France, rest day in Cannes;
attempted assassination of Togliatti, leader of the Italian
Communist Party; telephone call from prime minister De Gasperi

Left for dead that day, you stomped
the waterfront between the heels

and horn rims, wimpling head-
scarves, cigarettes as long as pens.

(Bullet one went high because
the hand was shaking; bullet two

passed through to exit at the flank;
the third lodged dirty in a lung.)

In the fanned hotel you watched
the waiters serving yellow

macarons. The call was routed
through from Rome; asked to be

the salve, you took your riders
to the waterline, streetlight's

spokes of silver on the black
bay's wheel. In the sand you drew

the next day's tactics, cols
and valleys like a cardiogram.

Selves

Tour de France, 1948; Stage 13, Cannes–Briançon, 15 July;
Tour de France, 1949; Stage 16, Cannes–Briançon, 18 July

Before you glimpsed him
on the Var, you thought you smelled

the camphor of his muscle rub,
the menthol of the oil

that was his second skin against
the cold – a lungful line of heat

that streamed away behind him
like a fox's scent. As the road

tore down, you saw him
in his turtle tuck, ordained him

in the lash of sleet as marker
for your line so that he seemed

yourself, flung forward by
the tour car's lights. You passed him

in the dark as second self; then
on the Izoard consigned him

to the past as scapegoat, portion
of your own despair cast out.

Pilgrim

Sanctuary of the Madonna of San Luca, Bologna; Giro dell'Emilia,
1952 (1ˢᵗ); 1953 (1ˢᵗ); 1954 (9ᵗʰ)

You took the ogee bend
at Orphan's Corner knowing

it was done. Whatever race
the others rode, yours now

was to the icon in the red
basilica, a devil's climb

away. In the archways
of the roofed arcade that lined

the hill, you saw your crumpled
brother on his buckled

bike, head turned towards
the crest beyond Nencini

and Defilippis. The whole road
emptied; you were kicking

clear, the years' grand massifs
shrunk to this: an incline

that was agony, sweet beeline
to a pair of almond eyes.

Summit

Funeral of Fausto Coppi, Castellania, Piedmont; 4 January 1960

They'd laid him out embalmed
on all front pages: pinstripe flannel,

rosary, his wife bent keening,
grasping at his slick, set hair.

His profile was a tour-stage
map – glazed lips the foothills,

peerless nose the final climb.
You noticed then how long

his lashes were, remembered how
in '48 you'd drawn up close near

La Rochelle to track the throbbing
of a vein. They bore him

over the raw fields, drifting up
in desultory black flocks. None of it,

you thought, was him: the studied
pace, the cold, the coffin ebony

and carved, the lack across those
gullied hills of anything approaching blue.

Farfalle

Giro d'Italia, 1991

Pitching up at start and finish
lines to clap them out

and hand them straw-tied
La Gazzetta sprays, you noticed

how the colour wheel had turned
from pastel shades to lustre,

block to pop-art *BOOM!* and
WHAM! They kettled you

in press pens, each year's
lanyard louder than the last.

Watching the kaleidoscope
roll in, you found yourself

again at Alfedena where, before
the bends, the leaders popped

their grey amphetamines
and cast the coloured wrappers

to the wind to play among
the pack like butterflies.

Gino Bartali: Palmarès

1935
1st, Road Race, National Road Championships
1st, Tour of the Basque Country
1st, Mountains Classification, Giro d'Italia
3rd, Giro di Lombardia

1936
1st, Giro d'Italia (and 1st, Mountains Classification)
1st, Giro di Lombardia

1937
1st, Giro d'Italia (and 1st, Mountains Classification)
1st, Road Race, National Road Championships
1st, Giro del Piemonte
1st, Giro del Lazio
2nd, Giro di Lombardia

1938
1st, Tour de France (and 1st, Mountains Classification)
1st, Tre Valli Varesine
2nd, Giro di Lombardia

1939
1st, Milan–San Remo
1st, Giro di Lombardia
1st, Giro del Piemonte
1st, Giro di Toscana
2nd, Giro d'Italia (and 1st, Mountains Classification)
2nd, Tre Valli Varesine

1940
1st, Milan–San Remo
1st, Giro di Lombardia
1st, Giro di Toscana
1st, Road Race, National Road Championships
1st, Giro di Campania
1st, Mountains Classification, Giro d'Italia

1941
2nd, Giro di Toscana
2nd, Giro del Piemonte
3rd, Giro dell'Emilia
3rd, Tre Valli Varesine

1942
2nd, Giro di Toscana
2nd, Giro di Lombardia
2nd, Giro del Piemonte

1943
3rd, Giro di Toscana

1945
1st, Giro del Lazio
1st, Giro di Campania
3rd, Giro di Lombardia
3rd, Tre Valli Varesine

1946
1st, Giro d'Italia (and 1st, Mountains Classification)
1st, Tour de Suisse
2nd, Giro di Toscana

1947
1st, Milan–San Remo
1st, Tour de Suisse
2nd, Giro d'Italia (and 1st, Mountains Classification)
2nd, Giro di Lombardia
2nd, Tour de Romandie
2nd, Giro dell'Emilia

1948
1st, Tour de France (and 1st, Mountains Classification)
1st, Giro di Toscana
2nd, Tre Valli Varesine
3rd, Mountains Classification, Giro d'Italia

1949
1st, Tour de Romandie
2nd, Giro d'Italia (and 2nd, Mountains Classification)
2nd, Tour de France (and 2nd, Mountains Classification)

1950
1st, Milan–San Remo
1st, Giro di Toscana
2nd, Giro d'Italia (and 2nd, Mountains Classification)

1951
1st, Giro del Piemonte
2nd, La Flèche Wallonne
2nd, Mountains Classification, Tour de France

1952
1st, Giro della Provincia di Reggio Calabria
1st, Road Race, National Road Championships
1st, Giro dell'Emilia

1953
1st, Giro di Toscana
1st, Giro dell'Emilia
3rd, Mountains Classification, Giro d'Italia

Glossary

Babbo	Dad
beretta	Italian-made pistol
bersaglieri	Italian infantry regiment
Bianchi	Italian cycling team (colours: blue and white)
bidon	water bottle
biretta	square, peaked cap worn by Catholic clergy
campionissimo	champion of champions: a title forever associated with Bartali's team-mate and then great rival, Fausto Coppi (1919–60), but applied also to others before him
coif	a nun's headdress
col	mountain pass
Corriere della Sera	'Evening Courier'; Italian newspaper, first published in 1876
dove sei?	where are you?
duomo	cathedral
farfalle	butterflies
fasces	a bundle of rods containing an axe; an ancient symbol of a magistrate's authority, coopted by Benito Mussolini's Italian Fascist movement
fraticello	little brother/monk
Giro d'Italia	Tour of Italy: annual multi-stage race, first held in 1909 to increase the circulation of the newspaper *La Gazzetta dello Sport*; with the Tour de France and the Vuelta a España, one of the three three-week-long European Grand Tours
Giro dell'Emilia	Tour of Emilia; annual one-day race in Bologna, first held in 1909
Giro di Toscana	Tour of Tuscany: originally a one-day, now a two-day, annual race first held in 1923
Giro di Lombardia	Tour of Lombardy, known as 'The Race of the Dead Leaves': the last of the five 'Monuments', or classic one-day races, of the season; first held in 1905
grappa	Italian grape pomace brandy
jaune	yellow; the colour of the overall leader's jersey in the Tour de France
L'Auto	daily French sports newspaper that originated the Tour de France stage race in 1903 to boost

	its sales; the colour of the jersey worn by the Tour's overall leader derives from the paper's yellow newsprint
La Gazzetta dello Sport	daily Italian sports newspaper, first published in 1896, that in 1909 originated the Giro d'Italia stage race to increase its sales; the colour of the jersey worn by the Giro's overall leader is the pink of the paper's newsprint
Legnano	Italian cycling team (colours: green and red)
loggia	covered exterior corridor or gallery
lunette	semicircular area decorated with paintings
maglia rosa	pink jersey; the overall leader's jersey in the Giro d'Italia
Milan–San Remo	annual race between Milan and San Remo in northwest Italy, known as 'The Spring Classic', the first of the five 'Monuments', or classic one-day races, of the season; first held in 1907
missal	book containing the service of the Catholic Mass
Moto Guzzi	Italian motorcycle manufacturer
mozzetta	ecclesiastical cape
musette	bag with long straps
nappa	soft sheepskin leather
osso buco	veal shin steak, including the circular bone and marrow
palmarès	list of 'palms' or prizes
parterre	ornamental garden with paths between the flower beds
peau	skin
peloton	the main group of cyclists in a race
putti	stout winged infants in Renaissance artworks
ragazzo	boy, lad
rochet	white, lace-trimmed ecclesiastical tunic
ruota	wheel
sett(s)	cobblestone(s)
soigneur	masseur, 'healer'
tifosi	(sports) fans
tondo	circular painting, mural or plaque
tor	rocky peak
Tour de France	Tour of France: annual multi-stage race, first held in 1903; with the Giro d'Italia and the Vuelta a España, one of the three three-week-long European Grand Tours

Acknowledgements and Afterword

Thanks are due to the editors of *Cunning Folk* (www.cunning-folk. com) and *Poetry Wales*, where some of the poems in this collection first appeared.

I am grateful, as ever, to Richard Marggraf Turley for shifting the gears on so many of these poems. I also thank Martin Kayman for s(t)age advice on everything from tablecloths to the properties of shadows. Warm thanks too to Zoë Brigley and Rhian Edwards, poetry editors at Seren.

I am indebted to a number of books that, from different perspectives and in multiple genres, profile Gino Bartali's career, life and times, the psychology of the professional racing cyclist and the cultures of the Grand Tours and classic one-day races knowns as 'Monuments' (then and now). Bartali's autobiographical collaborations with Mario Pancera; Romano Beghelli and Marcello Lazzerini; and Pino Ricci are key. Works by the following peloton of writers, historians, biographers, journalists and philosophers have been particularly valuable: Paolo Alberati; Andrea Bartali; Roland Barthes; Dino Buzzati; Michael Carver; Peter Cossins; Paolo Costa; John Foot; Alasdair Fotheringham; William Fotheringham; Max Leonard; Tim Krabbé; Aili McConnon and Andres McConnon; Benjo Maso; Richard Moore; Iris Origo; Alexander Ramati; Chris Sidwells; and Alberto Toscano. The reports of journalists from the 1930s to the 1950s, whose words have communicated the physical, mental, political and spiritual dramas of tours and giros, are often masterful pieces of imaginative writing. These races remain, as Hugh Dauncey and Geoff Hare put it, 'pre-modern contest[s] in a post-modern context'. They offered a stage on which the paradoxes of a man known as 'L'uomo di Ferro' (The Man of Iron), 'Ginettaccio' (Gino the Terrible) and 'Gino Il Pio' (Gino the Pious) could be publicly expressed.

In 2013, Yad Vashem (the World Holocaust Remembrance Centre) recognised Gino Bartali as 'Righteous Among the Nations' for his work as clandestine courier, throughout Tuscany and Umbria and as far south as Rome, of forged identity documents that saved the lives of hundreds of Italian Jews. He fulfilled these missions as part of a complex underground relief, resistance and rescue network, comprising Jews and Gentiles, operating under the umbrella of the organisation known as DELASEM – *Delegazione per l'Assistenza degli Emigranti Ebrei* (Delegation for the Assistance of Jewish Emigrants). Other organisers and members of the network, including the Cardinal Archbishop of Florence, Elia Dalla Costa (who enlisted Bartali), and those based in the counterfeiting centre of Assisi – Monsignor Giuseppe Placido Nicolini, Father Aldo Brunacci, Father Rufino Niccacci and the printer Luigi Brizi and his son Trento – had previously been similarly recognised.

Hagiographies are unhelpful; history (itself, necessarily, a narrativised assemblage) crucial. Recently, scepticism has been expressed (by Michele Sarfatti, among others) regarding Bartali's role in Dalla Costa's network and the Assisi Underground. While it is clear that certain myths have attached themselves to that period, the evidence and testimonies explicitly cited (and submitted to scrutiny) by Aili McConnon and Andres McConnon in *Road to Valour: Gino Bartali – Tour de France Legend and Italy's Secret World War Two Hero* (2012), pp. 281–90 are powerfully persuasive.

Bartali: the accent is on the first syllable.